SUPERSTARS
ULTIMATE STICKER COLLECTION

Read the captions, then find the
sticker that best fits the space.
(Hint: check the sticker labels for clues!)

Don't forget that your stickers can be stuck
down and peeled off again. If you are careful,
you can use your stickers more than once.

There are lots of fantastic extra stickers too!

London, New York, Melbourne, Munich, and Delhi
Written by Steve Pantaleo
Edited by Matt Buchanan
Designed by Carol Stamile
Production by Julie Clark
Published in the United States
in 2015 by DK/BradyGAMES
6081 East 82nd Street, 4th Floor
Indianapolis, IN 46250

15 16 17 10 9 8 7 6 5 4 3 2 1

Page design copyright © 2015 BradyGames

ISBN: 978-1-4654-3946-8

Printed and bound in China by L-Rex

Discover more at

www.dk.com

www.wwe.com

JOHN CENA

John Cena is the fearless leader of Cenation, his faithful legion of supporters. Over the past decade, Cena has been WWE World Heavyweight Champion more often than any other Superstar, earning him the nickname, "The Champ." No matter what the circumstances, Cena abides by the three-word code of Hustle, Loyalty, Respect.

THE CHAMP IS HERE!!!

DID YOU KNOW: Cena's first championship in WWE was the United States Championship. He won it by defeating Big Show at *WrestleMania XX*.

Constant weight training gives Cena the strength to lift Superstars twice his size!

John Cena never gives up. The greater the challenge, the harder he battles.

Cena has a special connection with his fans. "Let's go Cena!" chants from the crowd inspire him to stay true to his code.

DANIEL BRYAN

Daniel Bryan may look like an ordinary man to some. To others, he even resembles a goat, but never underestimate this bearded Superstar. Powered by the "Yes! Movement," Bryan battled his way to the main event of *WrestleMania 30* and won! Now, Superstars of all shapes and sizes must respect The Beard.

CAN I GET BACK TO THE MAIN EVENT OF WRESTLEMANIA? YES!

Daniel Bryan knows several submission holds, but none as lethal as the Yes! Lock.

The force of Bryan's Running Knee is a great equalizer against larger opponents.

DID YOU KNOW: Daniel Bryan is very eco-friendly. He once made a New Year's resolution to use the same water bottle for a full year to reduce waste.

Daniel Bryan riles up the crowd with one word—"YES!"

ROMAN REIGNS

A former enforcer of The Shield, Roman Reigns now fights for justice on his own with the same ferocity. The 2014 Superstar of the Year packs one of the most explosive offensive arsenals in WWE. He is equal parts strength and agility, making him dangerous to anyone in his path.

Reigns can smash through any obstacle with a Superman Punch.

A former football player, Reigns brings a smash-mouth style to the WWE ring.

Reigns intimidates foes with his intense glare.

DID YOU KNOW:
In 2014, Roman Reigns broke Kane's record for eliminations in a Royal Rumble Match, tossing twelve Superstars over the top rope.

DEAN AMBROSE

Dean Ambrose is unstable and unpredictable. Able to absorb and deliver punishment with the same gleeful tenacity, people often question his sanity, but never his ring skills. The Lunatic Fridge thrives on chaos, which he creates every time he steps through the curtain.

TO ME, YOU ARE THE CRAZY ONES!

Dean Ambrose plants another opponent with his Dirty Deeds finisher.

DID YOU KNOW:
Dean Ambrose was the longest reigning United States Champion in WWE history before losing the title in a 20-Man Battle Royal.

Several maniacal facial expressions all spell bad intentions for opponents.

Ambrose takes the action above the ring, on the ramp, and sometimes even in the stands!

SHEAMUS

With brute strength, a hot temper, and a warrior's spirit, Sheamus is one of the toughest competitors in WWE. His ancestors were the Celtic Warriors of Irish folklore. Sheamus has carried on this legacy by compiling numerous accolades in his WWE career, including multiple World Championships.

THERE ARE ONLY TWO THINGS I DESPISE —BULLIES AND THE SUN!

The famed Brogue Kick brings any match to a decisive end.

Fiery red hair and milky white skin give Sheamus a unique look.

DID YOU KNOW:
Sheamus won the WWE Championship in his rookie year, becoming the first Irish-born Superstar to claim the prestigious prize.

The White Noise finisher is one of many reasons not to mess with The Great White.

DOLPH ZIGGLER

Dolph Ziggler has jaw-dropping athletic ability. He knows it, too. Nicknamed "The Showoff," Ziggler loves nothing more than flaunting his skills for the WWE Universe. He also competes with tremendous heart. His gutsy performances over the years have transformed him into a fan favorite.

IT'S TOO BAD THAT I AM TOO GOOD!

The Zig Zag provides a thrilling conclusion to a show-stealing contest.

Dolph likes to look good while dazzling the WWE Universe with his ability.

DID YOU KNOW:
Dolph Ziggler held records as an amateur wrestler in both high school and college prior to joining WWE.

Ziggler's ability to grapple and leap through the air is a potent combination.

MONDAY NIGHT MEMORY LOSS!

WWE's announce team of Michael Cole, Jerry "The King" Lawler, and JBL is the best in the business. However, the mischievous Hornswoggle has slipped them a magic potion causing them to forget where each Superstar's image should go. Can you help them place the stickers as they call this *Raw* Battle Royal?

COLE: *That's right, especially with this exciting three-man team working together! The New Day has been on a roll since trying a new upbeat, positive outlook*

LAWLER: *This guy scares me, Cole...even without that creepy sheep mask!*

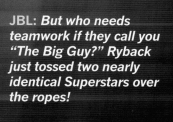

JBL: *But who needs teamwork if they call you "The Big Guy?" Ryback just tossed two nearly identical Superstars over the ropes!*

JBL: *Don't let his looks deceive you, Jerry. Erick Rowan is a bona fide genius with many artistic talents. And he will need those smarts to survive this Battle Royal.*

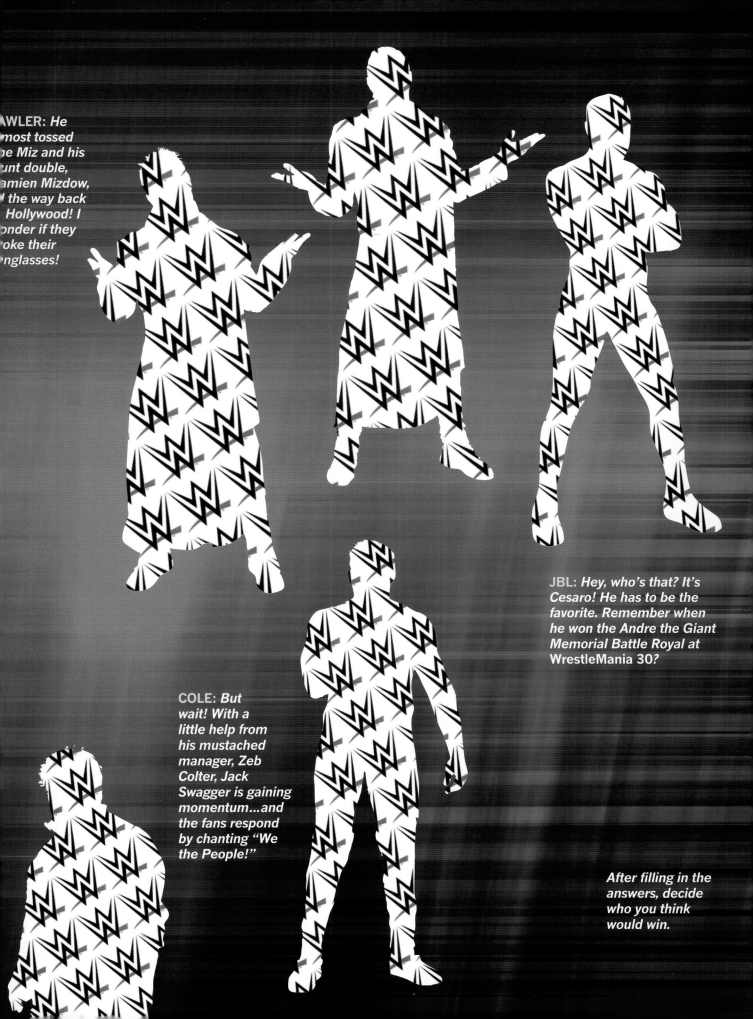

AWLER: *He
most tossed
he Miz and his
unt double,
amien Mizdow,
l the way back
Hollywood! I
onder if they
oke their
nglasses!*

JBL: *Hey, who's that? It's
Cesaro! He has to be the
favorite. Remember when
he won the Andre the Giant
Memorial Battle Royal at
WrestleMania 30?*

COLE: *But
wait! With a
little help from
his mustached
manager, Zeb
Colter, Jack
Swagger is gaining
momentum...and
the fans respond
by chanting "We
the People!"*

*After filling in the
answers, decide
who you think
would win.*

WHO IS WWE'S ULTIMATE SURVIVOR?

Each year at *Survivor Series*, Superstars form teams consisting of four or five members for thrilling tag team competition. Using the stickers from the back of this book, form your ultimate 5-on-5 *Survivor Series* Tag Team Elimination Match. Give each team a name. Decide what is at stake. Then predict the order of eliminations and decide who will stand tall after the bell!

Team Name_____

Members:

Team Name_____

Members:

If _____ *wins, then* _____

*must*_____*!!!*

Order of elimination:

Last Superstar(s) remaining:

Note that by Survivor Series rules, the match ends when all five members of one team have been eliminated. So you can have anywhere from one sole survivor to a clean sweep with the entire winning team remaining.)

HUSTLE, LOYALTY & RESPECT

John Cena faces incredible challenges nearly each week, but even against insurmountable odds, Cena never wavers from his code. Now he shares his tried and true formula for competing with hustle, loyalty, and respect!

Step 1: *"Your time is now! When that entrance music hits, it is time to focus. Get your game face on, but do not forget to acknowledge your rabid fans."*

Step 2: *"Respect your opponent's abilities, but have confidence in your own. Refuse to be intimidated or outworked by anyone."*

I'LL SEE YOU AT WRESTLEMANIA!!

Step 3: *"Never quit. Tell your rivals, 'You Can't See Me!' Then adjust their attitude!"*

IMPORTANT REMINDER!
John Cena and the WWE Superstars are trained professionals. Never try to copy their moves in the ring at home, in school, or anywhere else.

Step 4: *"You are the Champ! But remember—being Champ is a privilege, and with privilege comes responsibility. In my case, more hungry challengers!"*

BENDING THE RULES

Some Superstars will use some underhanded tactics to get to the top, even if it means the scorn of the WWE Universe. Here are some of the stars you love to hate!

BIG SHOW

Be careful around the World's Largest Athlete. He may seem like a gentle giant, but his devastating KO Punch has been used for devious means.

BROCK LESNAR

With the conniving Paul Heyman by his side, Brock Lesnar has one thing on his mind—destruction. He is merciless and believes he cannot be stopped.

DID YOU KNOW:
Brock Lesnar once hit Big Show with a Superplex that caused the entire ring to collapse under the weight of both behemoths!

BRAY WYATT

This Sinister Sermonizer believes in a darker purpose. He intends to lure others to his cause by brainwashing or by physical force.

TRIPLE H

The King of Kings is a legend of WWE. However, his heavy-handed ways since rising to power have earned him the ire of fans and Superstars alike.

RUSEV WILL CRUSH YOUR FAVORITE HEROES ONE BY ONE!

RUSEV

Flanked by the incorrigible Lana, Rusev is out to prove that he is superior to his American counterparts.

THE REIGN OF THE AUTHORITY

The power hungry heirs to Mr. McMahon's company have endured several threats to their mantle with the help of several devious minions. These Superstars toed the company line, whether it was "best for business," or for some ulterior motive.

SETH ROLLINS

The self-proclaimed Architect of The Shield betrayed his former brethren, buying into The Authority's cause. His deceit paid off when he claimed the Money in the Bank briefcase.

TRIPLE H & STEPHANIE MCMAHON

WWE's ultimate power couple was put in charge by the Chairman himself. They believe there is no WWE without them and will always seek to rule their empire with an iron fist.

RANDY ORTON

The deadly Apex Predator was handpicked by The Authority to be the "Face of WWE." However, he was later excommunicated from the inner corporate circle.

ORPORATE
ANE

e Big Red Monster still
rks inside him. However,
ese days the fiery demon
s donned a suit and serves
Director of Operations.

BATISTA

The Animal never considered
himself part of The Authority.
Still, his connection with
Triple H through their
Evolution partnership
puts him in good
graces with the powers
that be.

UKE HARPER

r being set free by Bray Wyatt, Luke
per provided some added muscle
Team Authority at
vivor Series.

MARK HENRY

The World's Strongest Man does not
need corporate backing. Still, when
push came to shove, he sided with The
Authority over John Cena.

DECORATE WWE HEADQUARTERS

DIVAS

The WWE Divas are some of the strongest, talented, and not to mention gorgeous women in all of sports and entertainment. Whether in the ring or backstage, these femme fatales are always looking for a leg up on the competition.

AJ LEE

The longest-running Divas Champion of all time has plenty to brag about, although her in-ring accolades speak for themselves!

NIKKI BELLA

A multi-time Divas Champion, Nikki is a cunning competitor who has proven several times there is no predicting what she has up her sleeve.

BRIE BELLA

Brie has proven to be her twin sister's equal throughout their turbulent relationship. When "Brie Mode" strikes, look out!

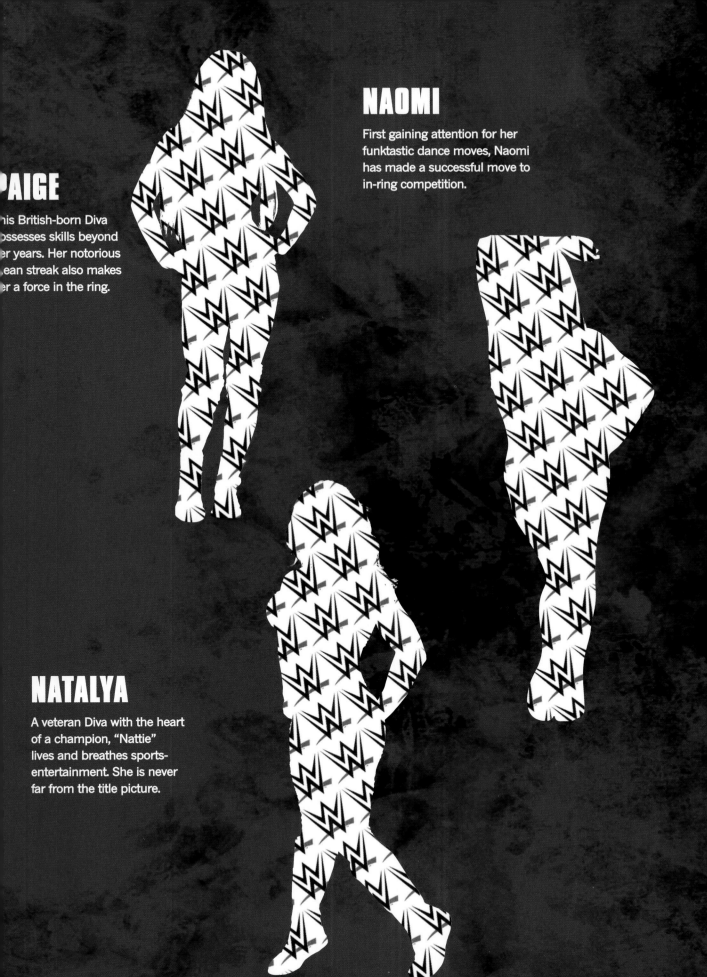

NAOMI

First gaining attention for her funktastic dance moves, Naomi has made a successful move to in-ring competition.

PAIGE

his British-born Diva ossesses skills beyond er years. Her notorious ean streak also makes er a force in the ring.

NATALYA

A veteran Diva with the heart of a champion, "Nattie" lives and breathes sports-entertainment. She is never far from the title picture.

LEGENDS

Long before Daniel Bryan was old enough to grow a beard, these WWE Legends blazed a path for today's Superstars to follow. Their prime years may be behind them, but their influence will be felt for generations to come.

ULTIMATE WARRIOR

A human comic book character, Warrior ruled the ring with face-painted intensity. He received an overdue Hall of Fame induction in 2014.

HULK HOGAN

Hulkamania ran wild in the 1980s. Decades later, the man in red and yellow still gets a thunderous applause when he puts his hand to his ear.

STING

The Franchise of WCW shocked the WWE Universe and The Authority by making his long-awaited WWE debut at *Survivor Series 2014*.

HE ROCK

e Rock returned
WWE in 2011 to
ove that he is still
st as electrifying
he was in the
titude Era.

SHAWN MICHAELS

A man of many
nicknames, HBK
always stole the
show, especially at
WrestleMania. Many
consider him the
greatest Superstar of
all time.

UNDERTAKER

The Deadman has wreaked
havoc in WWE for over two
decades. His 21-match winning
streak at *WrestleMania* will likely
never be equaled.

STONE COLD STEVE AUSTIN

As ornery as a Texas rattlesnake,
Austin still raises a ruckus
whenever he appears. When you
hear the glass shatter, watch out!

SUPERSTARS VS. LEGENDS BATTLE ROYAL

All WWE Superstars believe they are the best, but there is only one way to determine the true "greatest of all time." You decide! Set up the ultimate Battle Royal of Superstars past and present and choose the winner!

Participants:

THIS BATTLE ROYAL IS FOR A-LISTERS ONLY, LIKE ME!

FACE PAINT FIASCO!

The Usos are preparing to enter the ring. The only problem is they forgot their face paint! Get them ready for action by using pieces of their signature face designs from the stickers in the back of the book.

THIS IS STING!

In WCW, Sting began as a vibrant, bleach blonde powerhouse. Then he transformed into a darker, ghostly presence that loomed in the rafters of arenas. Now that this legendary enigma has finally emerged in WWE, there is no telling what he has in store. Evildoers beware!

THE ONE THING SURE ABOUT STING IS THAT NOTHING IS FOR SURE.

DID YOU KNOW:
Sting competed against "Nature Boy" Ric Flair on both the first and final episodes of *WCW Monday Nitro*.

Sting is a Superstar of few words. His stone-faced glare does all the talking he needs.

The explosive Stinger Splash brings the crowd to its feet.

The Scorpion Death Drop is one reason why Sting is a seven-time World Champion.

UNDERTAKER'S GRAVEYARD

Undertaker's illustrious Streak will go down in history as one of sports-entertainment's most legendary feats. Use the spaces below to fill in the graveyard for his 21 victims.

WRESTLEMANIA VII
Jimmy "Superfly" Snuka

WRESTLEMANIA VII
Jake "The Snake" Roberts

WRESTLEMANIA IX
Giant Gonzales

WRESTLEMANIA XI
King Kong Bundy

WRESTLEMANIA XII
Diesel

WRESTLEMANIA 13
Sycho Sid

WRESTLEMANIA XIV
Kane

WRESTLEMANIA XV
Big Boss Man

WRESTLEMANIA X-7
Triple H

WRESTLEMANIA X8
Ric Flair

WRESTLEMANIA XIX
Big Show & A-Train

WRESTLEMANIA XX
Kane

WRESTLEMANIA 21
Randy Orton

WRESTLEMANIA 22
Mark Henry

WRESTLEMANIA 23
Batista

WRESTLEMANIA XXIV
Edge

WrestleMania 25
Shawn Michaels

W*RESTLEMANIA XXVI*
Shawn Michaels

WRESTLEMANIA XXVII
Triple H

WRESTLEMANIA XXVIII
Triple H

WRESTLEMANIA 29

CM
Punk

BUT THE LEGEND OF THE UNDERTAKER WILL NEVER REST IN PEACE!

MY CLIENT, BROCK LESNAR, CONQUERED THE STREAK!

CREATE YOUR OWN
WRESTLEMANIA LINE-UP

WrestleMania 31 may be over, but Mr. McMahon is already hard at work planning next year's Show of Shows! Give the Chairman some help. Who knows, maybe some day he will put you in charge!

WWE WORLD HEAVYWEIGHT CHAMPIONSHIP MATCH

_____ VS. _____

w/ Special Guest Referee _____

STEEL CAGE MATCH

_____ VS. _____

_____'s Career is on the Line!

_____ VS. _____

w/ Manager_____

DIVA'S CHAMPIONSHIP MATCH

_____ VS. _____

_____ Match for the _____ Championship

_____ VS. _____

ADDITIONAL MATCHES

_____ VS. _____

_____ VS. _____

Featuring, the special host of *WrestleMania 32*

_____

YOU'RE HIRED!

Superman Punch

Ultimate Warrior

Triple H

Seth Rollins

Big Show

Erick Rowan

Luke Harper

Big Show

Naomi

Mark Henry

CENA APPROVED

Time To Focus

Lana

Brock Lesnar

Kane

Shawn
Michaels

Yes!

Paige

Kane

Constant Weight Training

Hulk Hogan

Cesaro

Never Quit

Snuka

Cena Never Gives Up

Rusev

Opponents Beware

Undertaker

The Miz

Edge

Zig Zag

Let's Go Cena

Cena Acknowledges Fans

STING

Sheamus

Zeb Colter

Natalya

Jake Roberts

Randy Orton

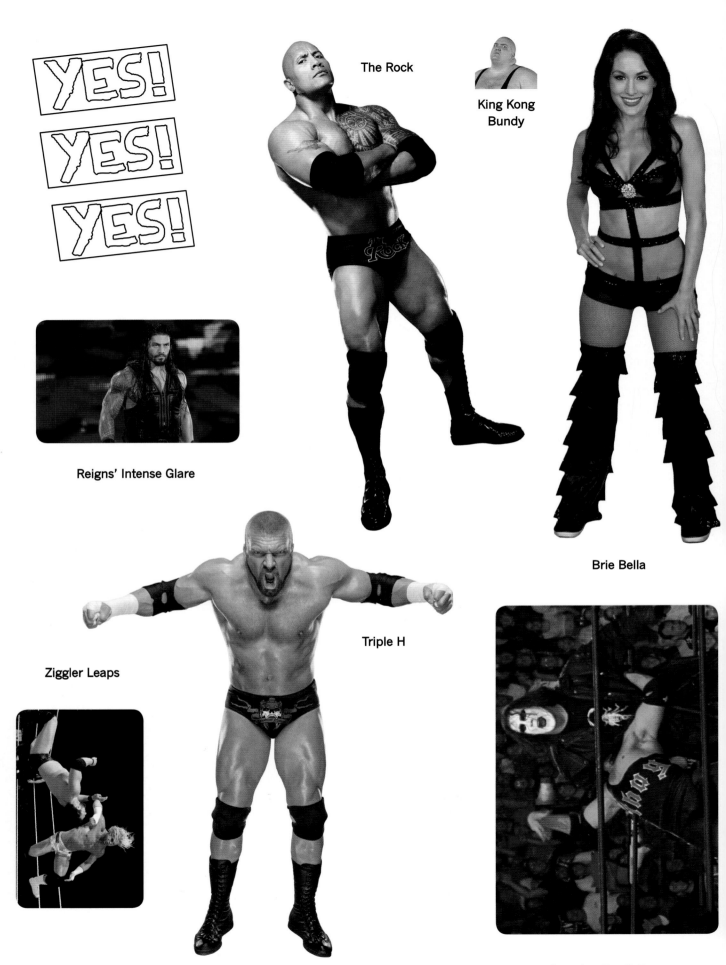

YES! YES! YES!

The Rock

King Kong Bundy

Reigns' Intense Glare

Brie Bella

Ziggler Leaps

Triple H

Scorpion Death Drop

Dean Ambrose

Stone Cold
Steve Austin

Stinger Splash

You Can't See Me

HBK

Dolph Ziggler

Stephanie
McMahon

Ryback

Batista

Refuse To Be Outworked

Sheamus' Unique Look

White Noise

The Usos' Face Paint

Bring On The Challengers

The Champ

Daniel Bryan

Big Boss Man

The Usos'
Face Paint

Ric Flair

Kane

Nikki Bella

A Superstar of Few Words

Roman Reigns

Jack Swagger

Running Knee

Above The Ring

Batista

HBK

Broque Kick

Randy Orton

John Cena

Dirty Deeds

Have Confidence

Diesel

AJ Lee

Triple H

Mizdow

Sting

Bray Wyatt

Yes! Lock

Triple H

Former Football Player

John Cena

Mark Henry

Sting

Triple H

New Day

Ziggler

EXTRA STICKERS

EXTRA STICKERS

EXTRA STICKERS

EXTRA STICKERS

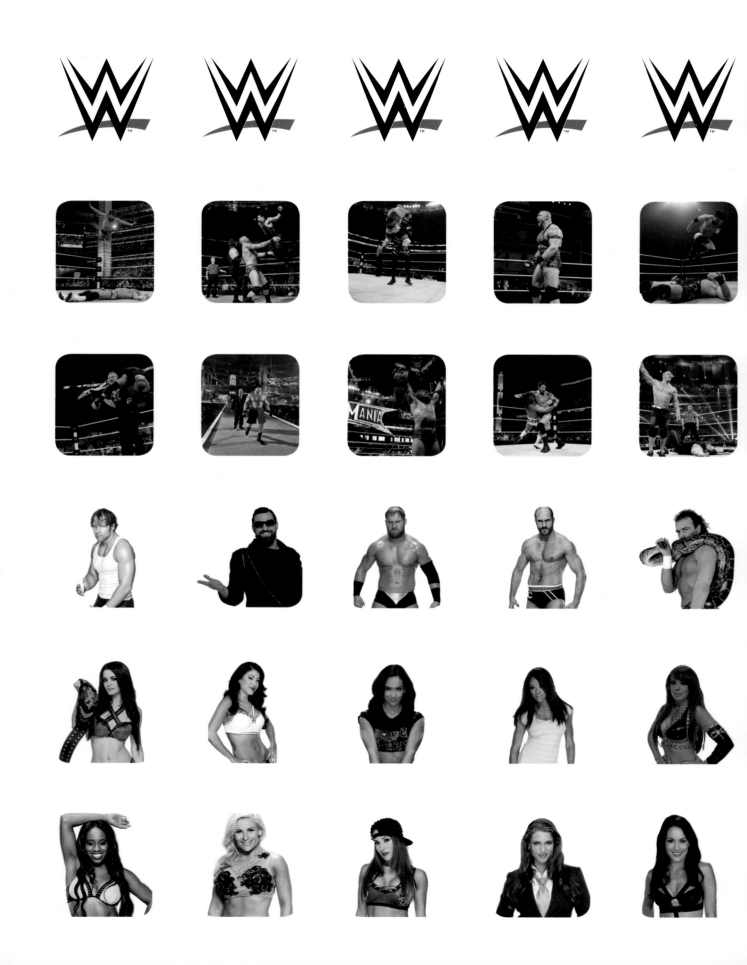

EXTRA STICKERS

EXTRA STICKERS

EXTRA STICKERS